*Pride and Pain
in Difficult Times*

Selected Poems

Pride and Pain in Difficult Times

Selected Poems

Basil Fernando
Introduction by K.G. Sankara Pillai

BELLE MARQUISE BOOKS
• NEW YORK, NY •

Copyright © 2017 Basil Fernando
Introduction Copyright © KG Sankara Pillai

All Rights Reserved

David Moratto, cover and interior design
Dhammika Heenpella, cover photo
Josefina Bergsten, author photo

No part of this book may be reproduced, for any reason, by any means, including any method of photographic or electronic reproduction without the permission of the publisher.

Distributed by Belle Marquise Books
New York, NY 10027
info@bellemarquisebooks.com

ISBN 978-0-692-83197-7

*This book of poems is dedicated
to the memory of my mother*

It was forty years ago.
As I left the building
where I used to teach,
I saw a rattlesnake
long and gloomy brown,
slowly moving down
in front of me.
When I reached your bed
in the hospital
it was empty.

Emptiness that came in then
would always be there, I knew.
I was thirty-two then,
the longest years with you nearby.
Forty years since then
are much shorter,
and there is much less to remember.

Long distance you travelled
great weight you carried,
the breath of your intelligence
is vivid before me
like a photograph,
and your voice, and the eyes.

Contents

An Appreciation of Basil Fernando's Poems . . . . *vii*

1	Yet Another Incident in July 1983	*1*
2	So There Was a War	*3*
3	Padma's Story	*4*
4	They Left her Lips in a Garbage Dump	*7*
5	Remembering	*7*
6	Drummers and Mothers	*8*
7	She Goes Looking for You	*9*
8	The Sea was Calm Behind Your House	*11*
9	Nandawathie's Son	*12*
10	The Courthouse	*13*
16	National Security	*14*
11	By the Wayside	*14*
12	The Faces	*15*
13	Mother and Son	*16*
14	Thoughts Rise Like Waves in a Rough Sea	*17*
15	Poison to the Soul	*18*
17	Mud Dies Giving Birth to a Lotus	*18*
18	A Woman for Other Women	*19*
19	My Lawless Motherland	*21*
20	Sambuka, The Low Caste Tapasa	*22*
21	A Son's Tale	*24*
22	Tell Me Dear Sister, Dear Brother	*27*
23	A Letter from Heaven for a Father Friend	*28*
24	A Poem for Godwin	*29*
25	A Father's Tale	*30*
25	Resurrection	*31*
26	An Old Man Sits Under a Tree	*32*
27	Each Swore by their Beliefs	*34*
28	Dear Birds	*35*

29	Its Beloved Awaiting	36
30	Come to Me	37
31	Come We Must Play — We Are Lovers	38
32	Like That Huge Mango Tree	39
33	Patriotism	40
34	On Ignorance	41
35	Those Who Have Nothing Interesting To Do	42
36	All Emptied Their Hands	43
37	Ekalavya, the Low Caste Archer	44
38	I am here, I will not Go Away	47
39	This Brotherhood of Evil I Reject	48
40	Then I Heard You Whispering in My Ear	48
41	*Mahaweli, Kelani, Walave, Kalu Ganga*	49
42	Kuweni the Queen	50
43	Fiftieth Year Get-together	51
44	She Forbids	54
45	To India	55
46	The River Behind the Bamboo Bushes	56

An Appreciation of Basil Fernando
K. G. Sankara Pillai

Sri Lankan poet, eminent jurist, and veteran human rights activist, Basil Fernando lives in Hong Kong, in exile. His life reminds me of Bei Dao who went into exile after the 1989 Tiananmen tragedy, and writers like Wole Soyinka, Dennis Brutus, Gao Xingjian, Mahmoud Darwish, and Taslima Nasrin in a galaxy of literary giants, artists and filmmakers whose works have been labeled by the authorities as subversive.

Friends of Black poetry are familiar with the theme of the return to the native land. Especially profound and far reaching is the impact of Aimé Césaire's *Cahier D'un Detour Au Pays Natal* (*Notebook of a Return to the Native Land*) in the development of a new sensibility of not only avant-garde Black poetry, but also an era of poetry of compassion and protest in the third world. A humanitarian poetic tradition with nerves of resistance, bones of protest, and the will to fight for freedom and equality. In Césaire's pioneering work, *return* is rediscovery, and the *native land* is the politico-cultural identity. A return to the native land is a return of the historical man engaged in the renewal of the self by participating uncompromisingly in the renewal of their world as creators of new meanings, apostles of resistance, and believers of the infinite possibilities of the human will.

Basil Fernando writes in Sinhalese and English. He works with friends from various parts of the world in his office at the Asian Human Rights Commission. He travels to far off places in history and jurisprudence, through labyrinths of the past and present, and into virtual and real spaces of the human experience. But all of Basil's journeys, and especially his poetry, return to Sri Lanka, his homeland. It is, however, neither a return to the past, nor a descent into nostalgia. Sri Lanka in

Basil's poetry is not a mythic island in the mysterious prehistoric whistles of the sea-breeze, neither is it the colonial Ceylon, tortured and looted by foreign invaders. Basil's element is the present reality of Sri Lanka with its violence, cries and resistance. The Sri Lanka of Basil's poems is a deep wound in the poet's mind; a bleeding face through which he must see, recollect, protest, and sing. A fragmented yet dazzling emerald to which his memory, dreams, and suffering are tragically attached and resurrected.

Justice is the most vital concern in Basil's poetry. He is a confident narrator of the times he has witnessed; his poems, children of a turbulent history of modern Sri Lanka and its demonically challenged dignity. It is writing destined to perform a crucial role in critiquing the deceptive powers of legislative, executive, judiciary. Basil's poems reiterate the fact that the real reason for human suffering is not fate; divine or metaphysical, but the merciless network of economic, political and historical capital and its manipulators.

Folk narratives have an organic hold in Basil's imagination. He brings forth many characters and situations from the past for a clearer articulation of contemporary disquiet. The source of images, characters, and references in Basil's poetry are folklore, fables and classical literature mainly from Sri Lanka and India. The poems Ekalavya, the Low Caste Archer and Sambuka, the Low Caste Tapasa, two Indian *Purana*[1] tales for example, are critically narrated to expose the foundation of injustice on which the Brahminical caste system is erected. Here the beast is the complex order of dharma, where even minor transgressions of traditional customs were punishable with inhuman torture and death penalties. Sri Lanka is the final destination of Basil's odyssey through the depths of contemporary world history. His roots lie deep in the Sri Lankan villages, in the lore and legends of the workers in the

---

[1] Purana Tales: Sacred Sanskrit texts containing Hindu myths, legends and folklore.

paddy fields and tea estates, and in the fairytales, mythology and memory of a great culture.

In *Mahaweli, Kelani, Walave, Kalu Ganga,* Basil asks himself, "What am I? What is my motherland?" But more than existential agony these questions convey the tragically uncertain predicament of his own society and its democracy. Basil's return to his native land in another sense is to recharge the belief that another world of values and justice is possible.

Words behave like rebels and warriors in Basil's poems. Through poetry Basil has sought to convey the pain and ignorance prevailing in his land, in every land. For him poetic expression is nothing less than the experience of what is historically valid, ethically essential, a popular form of enlightenment in times of chicanery and violence.

Basil's poetry is the poetry of an impassioned activist. An intimate reader of Basil Fernando's poetry can identify it as an authentic report of the polluted politics, imprisonment, torture, killings, disappearances, corrupted judiciary, denial of justice — history standing shockingly still amidst the ethical vacuum of brutal state power. Ultimately, Basil's poetry breathes justice: in the soul of its vision, its tone of historic urgency and the core of its spiritual energy.

Yet Another Incident in July 1983

Burying the dead
being an art well developed in our times,
Our psychoanalysts having helped us much
to keep balanced minds, whatever
that may mean,
there is no reason really
for this matter to remain so vivid
as if some rare occurrence.

I assure you
I am not sentimental, never having
had a "breakdown," as they say.
I am as shy of my emotions
as you are, and attend to my daily
tasks in a very matter-of-fact way.
Being prudent, too, when a government says:
"Forget!" I act accordingly.

My ability to forget
has never been doubted.
I've never had any adverse comments
on that score either.
Yet I remember
the way they stopped that car, the mob,
there were four in that car:
A girl, a boy
between four and five it had seemed
and their parents, I guessed, the man and the woman.
It was in the same way they had stopped other cars.

I had not noticed any marked difference.
A few questions in a gay mood,
not to make a mistake, I suppose.
Then they proceeded to action
by then a routine,
pouring petrol and all that stuff.

Then someone, noticing something odd
as it were, opened the two left doors of the car,
took away the two children
resisting and crying as they were moved
away from their parents.
Children's emotions have to sometimes
be ignored for their own good,
he must have thought.

Someone practical was quick, efficiently lighting a match.
An instant fire followed, adding one more
to the many around.
Around the fire they chattered
of some new adventure,
A few scattered.
What the two inside felt
or thought was no matter.

Peace-loving people were hurrying
home as if in a procession.
Then suddenly, the man inside the car,
his shirt and hair already on fire,
broke open the door.
Then bending, took his two children.
Not even looking around,
as if executing a calculated decision,
he resolutely re-entered the car.
Once inside, he locked the door.
I had heard that noise distinctly.

Still that ruined car is there by the roadside
with other such things.
Maybe the Municipality will remove it
one of these days
to the capital's garbage pit.
The cleanliness of the capital receives the Authority's top priority.

So There Was a War

So there was a war
Borrowing each day,
Borrowing more and more
Youth to die in the lines.
Luring them with smiles,
Luring them with songs,
And whichever way you like
Taking them to die.

Create a dream and a romance
Of this walk to be slaughtered,
Sing more songs after they die.
Tell the world,
"We did it all quite fine."
In remote villages, aged men and women
May mourn,
The rest of the nation is entertained
With fine songs.

Padma's Story

She sits by his bedside,
It is the sixth day since he fell into a coma.
Doctors express disheartening comments.
But to keep hoping,
and to sustain the hope of others
is perhaps the vigor of the eternal woman.

She pleads with the doctors
to keep the life machines on.
"No, it is not futile,"
she tells the medical men.
On the fourteenth day, her prayers are answered,
He opens his eyes.

She recalls the sheer madness;
Men in uniform grabbing
her husband and pushing him into a police jeep.
The next day, when she saw him
he could not stand.
Policemen apologizing,
"Mistaken identity."
She rushed him to a hospital just in time.

Supporting her were a few young persons
who call themselves Human Rights Activists
And a few of his fellow workers.
Three little children shocked and bewildered.
Some force rose from within her,
giving her strength
to console and comfort them.

Slowly she nursed him back.
In his smiles there was gratitude
like a blossoming flower.
She told him how police officers
had hung him on a beam,
assaulted him with iron rods,
commanding him to, "tell the truth".

He told the truth of his innocence,
they called him a liar
and continued to beat him.
Finally, they brought him down
Like Jesus from the cross.
Some officer applied balm,
telling him,
"We made a mistake".
His dignity hurt, he complained,
but doubted whether there would be justice.
Still wanting to pursue it, he went on
many journeys to court.

Then one evening came the news:
He was shot by the police.
Again, she returned to the hospital,
sat by him as he lay dying,
hoping for a miracle
that never happened.

That was ten years ago.
She raised the three children alone.
To keep them cheerful,
she hides her own agonies,
keeps up a smiling face.
Inside her is boiling anger
at the absence of justice,
absence of reason,
absence of humanity.
In her children she sees each day
continuing pain,
and many questions
that will never be answered.

On every full moon day,
She lays a lotus
at the Buddha's feet,
and prays that his children grow up
without bitterness
in their souls,
and that in the next birth,
he will be her husband again.

In 2002, a Sri Lankan man called Gerald Perera was arrested on mistaken identity, and beaten to an extent that he suffered kidney failure and fell into a coma, which lasted for over two weeks. After prolonged treatment and recovery, Gerald Perera pursued his complaints against the perpetrators, who were several police officers led by a Sub-Inspector. On the 26th of November 2004, while his case before the High Court was pending, before he could give his evidence, he was shot dead on a public bus. The Sub-Inspector and another suspect were charged with murder.

They Left Her Lips in a Garbage Dump

They left her lips
In a garbage dump.
He was left in confusion.
Incapable of anger,
He sought no revenge.
For years, he tried
To refix his mind,
But never succeeded.
He lived, body somewhere,
mind elsewhere.
All the time
Trying to fathom the riddle
Of the woman who was stolen.

Remembering

They say he is a warrior
They have brought him in a coffin.
I remembered the day I brought him
Bundled from the hospital.
All the village women were there
To assist me, and to see his face.

Drummers and Mothers

The drummer drums the war drum,
Bodies are blown away.
The drummer drums the war drum,
Brains are blown away.
The drummer drums the war drum
Minds are blown away.

At the palace, the drummer drums a festive beat,
There is dancing and singing,
The king is drinking deep.
Proud words flow from his mouth as water from a gutter,
Mothers move away to remote places
Their minds separate from their bodies.
They do not hear the drumbeat,
They do not hear or see anything at all.

She Goes Looking for You
A poem for Somchai Neelaphaijit

We go
Looking for you.
To be accurate,
She goes
Looking for you.
To be accurate,
She goes looking
For your bones,
Or for something that is yours,
A hair or a piece of cloth.
We are just the 'sub-committee'
Helping her
Find you.

We go to an abandoned house,
In an abandoned field.
We have forensics
Helping the 'sub-committee.'
Everyone is looking
For a piece of you.
Near the rubbish burning spot
Forensics find two piles of bones.
We think
We found you.

Forensics declare,
"Human bones."
We think
We found you.
The journey is yet long,
Spreading through fields
Through many more bones,
Through laboratories,
Jurists, and judges
Who must finally believe
That it is you.
She will go on that journey
Till she finds you.

The Sea Was Calm Behind Your House
A poem dedicated to M. I. Kuruvilla

On a day in July 1983
When our nation had gone mad,
I visited you.
The sea was calm behind your house.

You greeted me as before,
But something had gone wrong.
We both knew,
The measured silence we kept.

You were the master,
I was the child.
We had played that game before,
But that day it stopped.

Our cheerful beliefs shattered
We saw the unknown unfolding.
Fates smiling truant, the gods mocking,
The sea was calm behind your house.

Nandawathie's Son

I have waited for a revelation
explaining the death
of Nandawathie's son.
One night the village awoke
hearing the thunder of a shot
through the frail body of the young man,
People said from a gun
used to kill elephants.

Some said insurgents killed him
as he pasted posters for a rich politician.
Others say that it was another rich politician.
Story passed from mouth to mouth
Bewilderment still travels,
The affair still remains vivid.

The wonder still is
Whether he was as important as a president
Or a prime-minister
to warrant such an assassination,
This postal peon, Nandawathie's son.
She used to be at the Kovil[1]
Trying to interest the gods
In her children's hardships.

---

[1] Temple

The Courthouse

In a land called Injustice
In a place called City of Fear
There was a court presided over
by a man called Mr. Absurd.
The court sergeant was Mr. Drunkard,
The Mudilier was Mr. Bribery,
There were many clerks and peons
Who had no names.

The Litigants were the ordinary folk
who thought they had come to seek justice
about which
they had no notion.
Some thought it white,
Some thought it black.
Some as liquor,
And others as bribery.

In the appeals court
Mr. Absurd was held in high esteem,
The wisdom of Messrs. D and B
received the nation's applause.
Summons were never written,
but issued;
Fines never paid,
but consumed.
Mr. Absurd said
He held the balance,
Holding on to the shoulders
Of Mr. Drunkard and Mr. Bribery.

National Security

Even the stones pee
on hearing the name.
Birds forget how to fly,
flowers lose all smiles.
Mothers hide their children
as hens hide the young
sensing the evil eye of the eagle.
Grandmothers weep
gazing at photographs.

By the Wayside
Translated from Sinhala

This wreath
With no name attached
Is for you
Who have no grave.
As the place of earth,
Which embraced you
Could not be found,
This wreath was placed by the wayside.
Forgive me,
Forgive me
For placing a memorial for you
By the roadside.

Monument to the Disappeared, Waduwa Junction, Seeduwa, Sri Lanka

The Faces

In the sky
I sometimes see
Formations of
Faces
Now gone.
Once I saw
The spectacles
And cigarette
Of the one
I quarreled with
For years.
Even in dreams,
Before winning or losing
His life ended.
Eager to continue
I followed
The cloud,
But a harsh wind
Was pursuing him,
Shattering the image to pieces,
Suspending the debate
Yet again.

Mother and Son

You are always there
And you are not there.
I draw from you
Like a woman drawing water
From a well,
But I cannot touch you.

You are like a shadow,
My own shadow
I need you,
You do not seem to
Need me anymore.
But that is deception
I think.

Like the water and wall of the well
We are close to each other,
Yet I am apart like the wall.
I say, "Mother,"
You do not answer,
I know you are listening
Perhaps you are teasing me.

Thoughts Rise Like Waves in a Rough Sea

Destruction so immense
Losses to so many,
My own loss
Is infinite.
Inside my heart boils
Revenge, revenge, revenge.
"It is just,"
I am told
Again and again.

Mind creates designs,
"Just motivations purify
All evil,"
I am told
Again, and yet again.
Thoughts rise
Likes waves in the sea.
Over and over again
I weigh my designs,
My thoughts.

I learn to stomach the thought that
Justice transcends revenge.
Anger needs to forge a will
To do something better,
To dispel the power of evil
And not be its victim.

Poison to the Soul

Friend,
When people say
Look at the brighter side of things,
Shun them.
For such sayings are poison to the soul.
For in truth
Hope lies only in hopelessness,
When you know
The darker side of brightness.

Mud Dies Giving Birth to a Lotus

Mud dies giving birth to a lotus.
Each moment dies
Giving rise to thoughts
And roses of the heart.

Death, beauty and eternity
Are a single chain.
So is freedom and pain.
Cries of anger
Create the clean heart
Of a people, a nation.

A Woman for Other Women

Dressed in red, nine old men
wearing wigs sat looking down.
In the middle, in two rows sat
men and women, mostly young.
Around sat the onlookers
in the large hall of the Supreme Court.

One by one, those in the middle
walked to the microphone.
Each one read the solemn oath.
A young woman, dressed in a black gown
over her white sari and blouse,
In a clear, well-modulated voice,
read her oath,
bowed and returned to her seat
Proud and happy inside.

Years she had walked the Hulsdorf hills
full of ideas and dreams
that she would take her place
equal to everyone else.
To fight injustice, a woman warrior,
fearless and upright.
Listening to learned teachers,
debating within herself
What was right,
What was wrong.
In the books she read
about "the general will"
wondering what Rousseau meant.

All these pictures
rushed to her mind
as now she faced her client
lying in a hospital bed.
A forty-five-year-old mother of three,
gang-raped in the early morning
on her way to work,
Picked up by three-wheeler drivers.

What shall she tell those red-clothed men?
What do the books say?
What will bring justice
to this devastated woman?
Where is "the general will"
she wondered.

My Lawless Motherland

My lawless motherland
What am I to say to you?
Today, I saw the photograph
of this young woman
whose hand was severed by a thief,
A woman from Vavunia.
I also heard that the thief
shot her husband when he tried
to protect her.

Just yesterday I read about Doti,
a mother aged fifty,
speaking about the abduction and rape
of her seventeen-year-old daughter.
And that was at Kalutara
where the police protected
the rapist who works in the high court
not far from the police station.

My lawless motherland
What am I to say to you?

Sambuka, The Low Caste Tapasa

A grieving Brahmin
Carrying the corpse of his young son
Cursed Rama
And threatened a hunger strike
Unto death if the sin
That caused his son's death
Was not found and expiated.

Rama called his council,
Eight learned Rishis and Narada[2]
Who advised him
Of a Sudra
Aspiring to be a Tapasa,
And transgressing Dharma
By doing only what Brahmins should do.

Great Rama's duty
It was to find and punish
The evil doer and reassert Dharma,
Ending premature deaths
Among the twice born.
So promptly he set out
In his aerial car for the hunt.

---

[2] A Vedic sage

At last, in a wild region, Rama espied
A man practicing austerities.
Inquiring his genealogy,
Found the Tapasa was a Sudra,
A practicing Yogi aiming moksha,
Named Sambuka.

Great Rama cut off the Tapasa's head
Instantly without a warning,
Expostulation or any address.
For a Sudra deserved
No explanation, no pity,
Had no rights.

But even before the severed head
Fell to the ground,
The dead youth regained his breathing,
And Devas[3] descended from heaven
Singing Rama's praises.
Sages commended his action
And gifted a divine bracelet.

Such is the greatness
Of caste-preserving Dharma.
The divine justice of wrath
Against Sudras seeking holiness,
Crossing boundaries laid by Vedas,
Misconstruing as good what was evil.
Sadu, Sadu to Rama, the righteous avenger.

---

[3] Deities

A Son's Tale

It was a crowd of twenty or so
Many not-so-young, and some old.
One among the not-so-young rose,
This tale he told.

"Blame me not for what I say.
I am worried, and this I thought
I should loudly say
For years now it bothers me.
My father had a father,
Him my father dearly loved.
Humble and gentle a man was he,
I was told.
To a landlord's family,
A tenant farmer was he.

Working hard, earning but little,
With respect he served his masters.
Hurt in his heart he hid,
To his son he said:
Never a tenant-farmer be.
Get away from here and study.
To a distant place my father fled
With someone's help, books he read
After study some fortune he amassed.
During that long time
Of his father he did hear,
That the master, avenging the son's departure
Had beaten his father dear.

Some revenge my father had in mind,
Bought lands next to the master's.
Furious became this landed lot,
Seeing the servant's son their equal.

A day when we all were gone,
He was left alone
In the big house now he owned.
Some from the old master's house,
Like wolves entered and pounced
Beating him hard, shouting words so foul
Thinking him dead, happily left.
Returning home I saw my father dear
Thinking him dead, was full of tears.
With neighbours' help to hospital went
Found him unconscious but not dead.

Doctors did him well treat,
His heart did better beat.
All the story he did with names repeat,
Police and lawyers were upbeat.
Here my friends my worries start,
My father in fact breathed his last.
In court, three were sentenced to death,
I must say, I had my revenge.

Now do not blame when you this hear
Give me your forgiving ear.
When my father was still not dead
Here is something that the doctor said.
It is possible to prolong father's life a little,
But a serious surgery he needs.
There is a risk that his memory
He may fully lose.
I loved my father and his father too,
Wanted him alive with memory or not.

But with honesty let me say
A lawyer I did consult,
Briefly, this is what he said,
Your father has told what happened.
If he dies or lives to tell his tale
To death or jail or death those villians will go.
"If he lives but cannot tell his tale?"
I asked this lawyer and he said:
Then these villains will go free.
A profound problem in me arose.
The whole night sleepless I thought,
Justice for him, and his father I did want.
But to let him go,
That I did not want.

Tell what you wish or forgive if you can,
The risk of the loss of his memory
I did not take.
Soon peacefully he was gone,
Now my secret I have said."
Not-so-old man sat down.
There was silence all around
No word anyone uttered.

Tell Me Dear Sister, Dear Brother

Dear sister, dear brother
Kindly tell me,
How many petals
Make a flower?
How much smiling
A friend?
How much love
A lover?
How much tenderness
A mother?
How much sweat
A father?
How many bonds
A people?
Are oceans bigger
than love?
Mountains bigger
than emotions?
Dinosaurs bigger
than human commitments?
Skies wider
than expectations?
Dear sister, dear brother
Kindly tell me,
How much anger
Should there be
When injustices destroy
all this that is human?

A Letter from Heaven to a Father Friend

Here in heaven
I told the Divine One
I wish to exchange the seventy-two virgins
Given to the martyrs
For the gift of compassion.
And the Divine One smiled at me
As you, my father-friend, used to do,
And granted me my wish.

So I look once again to the world,
My family and friends,
And you, my father-friend with the playful eyes.
I do not suffer any more with petty traits of hate or revenge,
With you, my father-friend, there are few words to exchange.

In your mind you have this fancy
That I am a vengeful son.
This, my father, is a poor assessment of me,
I am your son.
The baby smiles I had,
I have them still, now eternally.
Look on me with love,
Do not think of me as a vindictive fool
But the greatest lover, loving you everlastingly.
Do not insult my memory,
Trust my wisdom
Ever-wanting our father-friend linkage.
Love me,
Do not fear me.
Love me,
Do not fear me.

A Poem for Godwin

In pouring rain
We took you from home
To grave, last April.
Just three years earlier,
Still fat and happy,
You went to hospital
Accompanied by our sister,
Telling your two little sons
You'd soon return.
This April, there're sour oranges
On the tree you planted,
And mangoes on the tree in front.
Two sons throw their reports
At us, making us proud.
In their eyes however, we see
Ever growing worry
Over the finality of your absence.

A Father's Tale
A poem dedicated to Dr. Manoharan

I had a son
I belonged to a nation
And the nation killed my son.

"Shoot to kill" is law for some
Loving a son is nature's law.
Who is who, what is what,
Which is which, I no longer know.

My neighbours' ears are waxed,
Eyes tightly closed
forget my son, I am told.

Am I insane?
Or is my nation insane?
To love and mourn a son
Is that a national shame?

"Shoot to kill" is law for some
Loving a son is nature's law.
Who is who, what is what,
Which is which, I no longer know.

Resurrection

Today I talked to a man
Who had escaped
A death camp.
Resurrection?
No,
He is dying now.

Growing thin
Looking dazed and haggard
Having nightmares,
Mentally not all there.
"Typical signs
Of those who undergo
Such experiences," says the psychiatrist.
Is there any typical sign
To know what
His torturers go through?

Sweet dreams, nice children.
Great hopes?
I could have helped
This man to escape
The dreaded camp.
I am powerless now
To prevent his slow death.

An Old Man Sits Under a Tree

An old man sits under the shade of a tree
On the slab of a grave.
He is no sage
Running away from world,
He was the grave digger
Now in retirement
Returning to a familiar world.

The only interludes are the night visits
Back home for his drink, dinner and sleep.
In his dreams he moves into the underworld
Of Hades, Lucifer or Yamaraja.
Sometimes seeing the faces of those
He buried.

The cemetery is place of ceremonies,
Of emotions, a powerful world
Where love is dramatized
And people become real.
Tears, loud cries, explosive words,
Flowers and candles trying to express
The language of the heart.

Unforgettable cries of mothers
When the young are buried,
Children saying goodbye
To their mothers and fathers,
A place where intellect is silent.

Then there are the unusual times
When men in uniform
Come with gallons of illicit liquor
And vehicle-loads of wounded dead bodies.
Preparing rapid fires
In the dead of the night,
To bury all the secrets
As more uniformed men
Guard the gates.

As the days go by
Visits by relatives,
Many questions.
Between heaven, hell and earth
With Angels, devils and spirits
Sits this old man,
His mind confused with facts
Fabrications and fantasies.
Images of thousands of faces
Confused about fate, faith,
Truth, justice and despair.
Hypocrisy, disorder and fear,
And tales of a thousand varieties
Crowding in his mind.

Each Swore by Their Beliefs

Some went crazy,
Declaring that killing is the way
To liberation.

Then soldiers declared
That killing the liberators
Is the path to liberation.

Each swore by their beliefs,
Killing was talked of as the ideal.
People passed dead bodies,
Not wanting to find out who they were.

Killers and the killed
All were neighbors.
Unable to make out
What it meant to love
One's neighbor,
Sanity and lunacy
Became indistinguishable.

Dear Birds

Dear birds,
From the sky,
From the treetops
You see a lot.
Perhaps a lot more than
What we see,
Me and my like.

I have always wanted
To see things as you do.
Now, tell me,
Spare a moment to tell me.
Do you remember
Everything you see?
When you rest at night,
Do you try to make out
What you have seen?
What have you witnessed?

Its Beloved Awaiting

As I listened
To the thick darkness
Of the night,
Disturbed by the casual conversation
Of night birds,
I heard the thin river
Moving on slowly
With some secret purpose
Deeply hidden within it.

Rather hostile to me,
Complaining
Of my unwanted intrusion
Of my insensitive judgment
Against its pain-ridden,
Long-enduring love,
In the thick darkness
Its beloved awaiting.

Come to Me

Tonight
when my soul is sad
among the darker things,
lonely,
Send to me
in the shadowy dark
the shadow
Of your fleeting being.
Your being
Like the self-effacing
gold
of the twilight,
moving slightly
in the evening sky
To awaken me
To the mysterious light
Of the night.
To move me
Among the unmoving things
Towards things ongoing,
Unending.

Come, We Must Play — We are Lovers

Please do not amuse yourself
By trying to put me off
Saying, I am dead or I am in prison.
Come, come, do not say such foolish things.
We are late, come let us go and play.

Let us run around in the field,
Go after grasshoppers and butterflies.
Or let us go to the pond,
And watch young tortoises swim,
And those long red fish with white bellies
Floating like kites.

So many things to do and say.
Come, come, stop pretending.
Ok, if you are dead, now it is time to wake up.
If you are in prison, just break the gates and come.
We must play my friend, do not delay,
We are friends, we are lovers.

Like That Huge Mango Tree

You exist
You are real
This is not a dream
But the knowledge of
My inner being.

You exist like that huge mango tree
That was in front of our house,
Gifting thousands of fruits each year
Housing squirrels, and hundreds of birds.
That tree lives within me
More real to me than the mini-trees,
That are everywhere these days.

You, my childhood neighbors,
Hardworking men and women
With those loud laughs,
Ever deep looks of compassionate eyes,
Yes, you are very much alive.

Patriotism

In cold-blooded calculation
A bird sings a song of gratitude
To the land that produces
Such delicious worms.

So do politicians celebrate the land
That produces such fools
Who let them hold on to power.
Thoughts of sweeter ages,
Like fairy tales
Where neighbours loved neighbours,
Judges protected citizens.

Mothers were more important than others,
Little dogs, little boys, little girls and angels were friends.
All of this rushed to my mind.

On Ignorance

"How many ships go on the sea,"
He asked,
I said I did not know.
"How many come to our harbor,"
He asked,
I shook my head.

"You think two million rupees is a lot?"
He asked,
Referring to the bribe
He is said to have taken
From someone transporting illegal immigrants.
"Yes, of course," I said,
"It is nothing, it is nothing,"
He said
Contemptuously, laughing
At my ignorance.

Those Who Have Nothing Interesting to Do

The problem with many people
Is that they seem to have
Nothing interesting to do.
Let me give one example.
My neighbor's hen
Looking for good place
To lay her egg
Chose another neighbor's bed.
A child, unaware of the intricacies
Of ownership,
Took the egg, and used it as ball.
The egg broke,
He was disappointed, so he cried.
The neighbor who owned the hen,
Accused the child's mother of theft.
She in turn blamed the owner
For allowing the hen to trespass.
Both started shouting at each other
And this lasted a long time.
Someone else reported the quarrel
To the police,
And the police filed a case before the magistrate
Who remanded both parties
To ensure peace.
This was a year back
And the case is still pending.

All Emptied Their Hands

I saw a procession of people
In a dream.
Their fists were closed,
And it looked like they were
Carrying something.
"These are the hypocrites and bullshitters",
A voice told me.
Each came to the pot,
Looking like a ballot box,
All emptied their hands
And left.
Then someone opened the box,
Maybe for counting I thought.
Then the box was emptied,
"Alas, there is nothing!"
The same voice said.

"Andi Hath Denage Katava" is a popular story of seven Brahmins who went on a journey. At night they met on a wayside resting place. They tried to make dinner where each Brahmin went to the water pot with a closed fist and emptied it. However, when dinnertime came there was nothing but the boiling water.

Ekalavya, the Low Caste Archer

Art of the arrow
Can't be borrowed
From Guru to Guru.
The law said in a narrow line,
This be imparted.

He was young
Of eternal laws ignorant.
Dreamed day and night
To be a swift dispatcher of arrows
To heaven and to hell.

"Not for us, my son
This art.
For Vedas has made us low caste
Archery is for higher caste,
Suffering for lower caste."
Mother told the boy.
"Besides gurus demand Dakshina
Only the rich can give.
Those who steal knowledge
They do not forgive."

From afar the boy watched,
Hiding often in trees,
How the Guru taught his boys,
And secretly doing the same.
"Oh, what a joy!"
Soon it was simple play,
Every move he could display.

An image of the guru in wood he made,
Before playing, prayed.
Once when meditating
Heard a dog barking.
Sent a small arrow
To where the noise was,
Lightly closing dog's jaws.

The Guru and trainee prince passing
Marveled at what they were seeing.
Was some god in jest
Their hard learning belittling?
Guru sadly wondered,
And looking around, saw a boy praying
Before an image so like his.
Then in a flash realized what was happening.

"If I be your guru
My Dakshina now give," he demanded.
"Money and gold I have none
Great sir! But even my life
I will give to learn from you
The art of the arrow,"
Unwise boy said.

For generations learned in cunning
The Guru smiled promising,
"Your left thumb be the Dakshina,
In exchange I will teach you
The art of the arrow."
Swiftly guru gave the knife
Swiftly boy obeyed.

The thumb he accepted,
And quickly he departed
Having protected his art.
Old tale here ends,
But may I add,
If I was that lad
A different end
This tale would have had.

I Am Here, I will Not Go Away

You listened to me
With fingers plugged in your ears.
That I should not speak
Was the unwritten rule.

But I did, and quite a lot
And you closed your ears.
It is not my voice you disliked
But that I had spoken.

It disturbed your world view
I was an intruder,
But I am here, I will not go away.
Keep your ears plugged as long as you like.

I am here, and I am speaking,
Speaking, speaking, no matter how long.

This Brotherhood in Evil I Reject

You say we are brothers
And we have a common enemy.
You come with blood on your hands
To prove to me you are fighting for me.
As brothers we must jointly hate the other,
You tell me.
In hate what brotherhood
Can there be?
Must I teach my child to hate
The way you say you do?
This brotherhood in evil I reject,
This I will not teach.

Then I Heard You Whispering in My Ear

You the silent one, you are the people.
I came from your womb,
You broke my silence.
You the motionless one, you are the people.
I came from your womb,
You made me mobile.
I have talked, I have moved,
I have felt the separation.
I have become silent, I have become immobile.
Then I heard you whispering in my ear:
Arise and walk, for we are moving.
Arise and talk, for we are regaining our hearing.
So I arose, I heard you talking and myself talking too.

Mahaweli, Kelani, Walave, Kalu Ganga

I used to sing
kavi from padyawaliya
Mahaweli, Kelani, Walawe, Kalu Ganga
flowing from the butterfly hill.
Heard songs also of ratharan puthun,
and charming girls growing up in the villages.

Then I saw
bodies floating in rivers,
rainwater mixed with blood
flowing from mountains,
floating bodies
eaten by kabaragoy.

Now, I do not like to hear of
Walawe, Kelani, and Kalu.
Mountains have lost
mystery or attraction.
In the eyes of mothers,
I see not tears but distrust.

What am I? I ask myself,
What is my motherland?
I want to sing those poems,
to that I can't bring myself.

Kuweni the Queen

She was queen of all birds,
elephants,
plants and flowers,
And all seeds.

She did not tame elephants
To fight wars or to be slaves.
She did not cage birds
Nor enslave her brothers and sisters.

Seeds were birthed and gave birth,
Birds sang, and there were more birds,
Elephants roamed and created more such giants,
And Kuweni, their queen, was a queen of love.

Sun shined and rain rained,
Winds blew and, at times, rivers flooded.
With love and care she managed it all,
She was the mother, the friend, the woman, the queen.

To Kuweni's land came the looters,
Vijeya, Don Lorenzo de Almeida and others.
They did not come to settle and share,
But to battle and take
Whatever was there.

Spirit of love and care
Was now no more fair.
The queen was crushed
Her people ambushed.

Murder was introduced,
Cheaters triumphed.
Looters were crowned,
Kings became clowns.

Kuweni's blood still survives,
Her sprit still lives
Like those of the trees, bushes and birds
That even in adverse weather survive.
Her song can still be heard,
In a rainbow, she reappears.

Kuweni is the mythical queen of Sri Lanka's original people. Vijeya is the mythical first invader of Sri Lanka. Don Lorenzo de Almeida, arrived in Sri Lanka in 1505, and is recognized as a brutal Portuguese invader. With him began the Portuguese conquest of part of the Maritime Provinces in Sri Lanka, which lasted for 150 years. The Portuguese were followed by the Dutch, and the British who conquered the whole island. Sri Lanka regained independence in 1948, but local rulers have failed to guarantee freedom to the local people.

Fiftieth Year Get-together

My little country, Pearl of the Indian Ocean
Paradise Isle: Portuguese, Dutch, British knew,
drank tea, feasted in Lanka, Sri Lanka.
Illiterate women making love
to illiterate men
made this land, my land, flow with honey.

For 50 years, my land, my lungs full
of fresh air,
Rice, smiles, kisses.
Tears too, tens of thousands
disappeared, bombs,
bullets, child prostitutes and soldiers.

I wonder about
reading histories, seeing
photographs, other people's
Stalin/Koba/SoSo/Joseph
bloodied humans like millions of flies.

Pol Pot not unequal,
Asian blood rivers,
Indonesian, Indian corpses.
I try to pray, I am Christian.
I try to meditate, my heritage is Buddhist.
Each day is All Souls' Day.

No gold medals for Stalin,
yet imitators everywhere.
Fear, they believe, is necessary for peace.
The Berlin Wall fell,
Now they shoot only immigrants.

"Hail Mary," my 7-year-old girl
says, "Father, say with me Hail Mary."
Why disappoint a child? I join her.
I was like her too,
I pleaded to the whole white heaven,
Hail Mary, do hear our people's cry.

Fifty years of prayers,
How can I tell my child they do not care?
No, I have joined in her prayers.
Hail Mary, stop my land's bleeding,
Jesus join us for tea in Buddha's land.
Me and my child will join you anywhere; just stop the killers.

Maybe we can play games when we meet,
put on masks: we become white,
You brown.
We know your crucifixion,
feel for you very much.
Take a turn if you like and get to know ours.

My little girl is funny,
She may ask questions.
Sometimes she asks me,
"Father, can't we abolish hell?"
"Lots of people will oppose us," I tell her.
You may like our games, really!
Very innocent, childlike,
no tricks, no cheating.

She Forbids

She forbids
Me
To dwell
Within
Her majestic dimensions.
Forbidden
I go, a wanderer,
Homeless.
In her dwelling
I
As a stranger treated,
I cry
Homesick.
Things passing
Bring no news.
No solace
My cry to convey,
No messengers allowed.
Walled out,
I cry in the street
Homesick.

To India

No patriot by inclination,
I didn't know where I belonged.
But when I visited you,
I knew who I was.
Little land is no land,
Little life is no life.
And to the size of my thought,
you are the sole companion.

It isn't the past,
It isn't the present.
It isn't the Gandhis',
The Nehrus' or even
Subhash Chandra Bose!
It cut you into two,
The history,
And I bleed daily.

Who will heal me?
Who will understand me?
But something tells me within,
Of some great deed,
Of some act
Aspiring to unity,
Be Born. Be Born,
My Motherland.
Be Born to Thy Unity!

The River Behind the Bamboo Bushes

Behind the bamboo bushes
There is a path
Leading to the river.
In the river there are
A lot of things
To think about.
Thoughts of you flow
From the river to me
And me to the river.

From this river thoughts flow
To the longer river of life,
And from that long river
Thoughts flow back
To this river.

Behind the bamboo bushes,
In that to and fro
You are there, in a million ways
Taking me back to where everything began,
Every sorrow, every tear,
Every woman, every man, every child.
Behind the bamboo bushes,
In the path leading to the river,
I walk holding your hand
Holding the hands of everyone.

About the Author

Basil Fernando is a leading global human rights activist, jurist, author and poet. He is the recipient of the 2014 Right Livelihood Award, Kwangju Prize for Human Rights, editor of *Article 2* magazine, and has been a Senior Ashoka Fellow. Following a career as a human rights, labour and criminal lawyer with the Sri Lankan Supreme Court, Fernando was inspired by the life and work of Indian statesman Dr. B.R. Ambedkar and Danish philosopher N.F.S. Grundtvig to embark upon a lifelong crusade to defend human rights. With the outbreak of the Sri Lankan civil war, Fernando was further thrust into a pivotal role in addressing judicial breakdown across Asia.

He has served as Appeals Counsel for Vietnamese refugees in Hong Kong, which was sponsored by the United Nations High Commissioner for Refugees (UNHCR), and as Senior Human Rights Officer-In Charge of the Investigation Unit under the UN Transitional Authority in Cambodia (UNTAC). He was also Officer in Charge and Chief of the Legal Assistance at the Cambodia Office of the UN Center for Human Rights. He is currently Director of Policy and Programme Development at the Asian Human Rights Commission in Hong Kong, and Executive Director of Asian Legal Resource Centre (ALRC).

Fernando has authored numerous works on human rights and legal reform including, *The Right to Speak Loudly: Essays on Law and Human Rights*, *Problems Facing the Cambodian*

Legal System, Modernization vs Militarization: Ethnic Conflict & Labour in Sri Lanka, Power vs Conscience, Sri Lanka's Dysfunctional Criminal Justice System and Gyges' Right: The 1978 Constitution of Sri Lanka. He is co-author of *The Phantom Limb* and has co-edited books including *Decline of Fair Trial in Asia.* He has also contributed numerous articles to academic journals, magazines and newspapers.

www.ingramcontent.com/pod-product-compliance
Lightning Source LLC
Chambersburg PA
CBHW032049290426
44110CB00012B/1021